Tiptoe Into Scary Places

Haunted Playgrounds

by Rachel Rose

Consultant: Debbie Felton
Professor of Classics
University of Massachusetts
Amherst, Massachusetts

BEARPORT PUBLISHING

Minneapolis, Minnesota

Credits

Cover, © Kim Jones, © Triff/Shutterstock, and © Torychemistry/Shutterstock; 3, © akids.photo.graphy; 4-5, © Kim Jones, © lordn/stock.adobe.com, © Monkey Business/stock.adobe.com, and © Andrea Izzotti/stock.adobe.com; 6, © Stan Reese/ Shutterstock; 7, imgur.com; 9, © Nicolai Kazakov/Shutterstock, and © Dillon Naber Cruz/Shutterstock; 11, © Google Maps; 12, © Joe Therasakdhi/Shutterstock; 13, © Lightspring/Shutterstock; 15, © AmityPhotos/Alamy and © Liviu/Shutterstock; 16, © chippix/Shutterstock; 17, © AmityPhotos/Alamy; 19, © EduardoCarneglia; 20, © elina.nova/Shutterstock and © Vcoscaron/Shutterstock; 21, © Albert Yarullin/ Shutterstock; 23, © Robnroll/Shutterstock; and 24, © krystal dollery/Shutterstock.

President: Jen Jenson
Director of Product Development: Spencer Brinker
Editor: Allison Juda
Designer: Micah Edel
Cover: Kim Jones

Library of Congress Cataloging-in-Publication Data

Names: Rose, Rachel, 1968– author.
Title: Haunted playgrounds / by Rachel Rose.
Description: Minneapolis, Minnesota : Bearport Publishing Company, 2020. | Series: Tiptoe into scary places | Includes bibliographical references and index.
Identifiers: LCCN 2020002535 (print) | LCCN 2020002536 (ebook) | ISBN 9781647471743 (library binding) | ISBN 9781647471804 (ebook)
Subjects: LCSH: Playgrounds—Juvenile literature.
Classification: LCC BF1477.25 .R66 2020 (print) | LCC BF1477.25 (ebook) | DDC 133.1/22—dc23
LC record available at https://lccn.loc.gov/2020002535
LC ebook record available at https://lccn.loc.gov/2020002536

For more information, write to Bearport Publishing, 5357 Penn Avenue South, Minneapolis, MN 55419. Printed in the United States of America.

CONTENTS

HAUNTED PLAYGROUNDS

The children have all gone home, and you are alone in the playground. You hear a soft rustle behind you. When you turn, no one is there. Suddenly, you hear a creak, and a swing slowly starts to move—by itself!

Get ready to read four spooky tales about playgrounds. Turn the page . . . if you dare!

GRAVEYARD GHOSTS

Dead Children's Playground, Huntsville, Alabama

The playground in Maple Hill Park lies hidden away—inside a **cemetery**! The little playground's swings and jungle gym are busy during the day. But it's what happens at night that has earned it the nickname Dead Children's Playground.

More than 80,000 bodies are buried in Maple Hill Cemetery.

Dead Children's Playground

At night, people have heard **phantom** children laughing and calling out. Swings have been seen moving by themselves. Strange, glowing orbs of light float in the night air.

Who are these unseen visitors? Some say they are the spirits of children who were kidnapped over 50 years ago near where the playground is today.

DEMON BOY

Fox Ridge Playground, Henderson, Nevada

The spooky fun begins around midnight at Fox Ridge Playground. People say that is when a swing there starts to move by itself.

The **legend** of the playground tells the sad story of a little boy who was hit by a car nearby. People believe it is his ghost playing on the swing.

Fox Ridge Playground

Some people say they've seen the young phantom wandering around the playground. But once the spirit realizes he's been seen, he quickly vanishes. Local children claim he turns into a **demon** before he disappears!

Perhaps the boy isn't the only phantom to haunt the playground. Some have reported seeing other spooky, shadowy figures at night.

HAUNTED ATTRACTION

Pennhurst State School and Hospital Playground, Spring City, Pennsylvania

Pennhurst first opened in 1908. It was both a school and a **psychiatric** hospital. The **patients**, many of them children, were treated badly there, and some of them died. The hospital was closed in 1987. Its nearby playground is neglected and overgrown. However, some say the spirits of former patients still haunt the place today.

Pennhurst State School and Hospital Playground

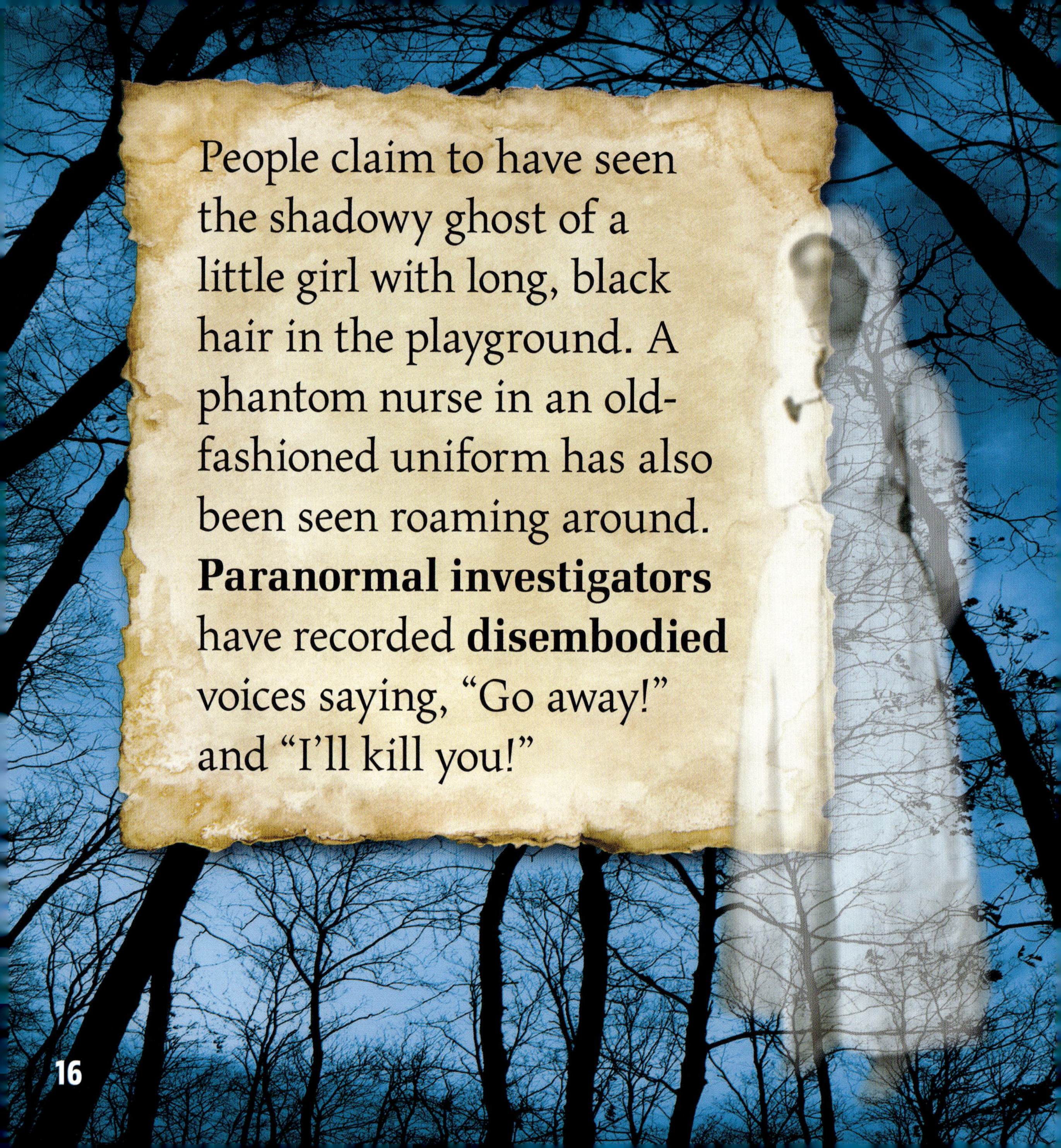

People claim to have seen the shadowy ghost of a little girl with long, black hair in the playground. A phantom nurse in an old-fashioned uniform has also been seen roaming around. **Paranormal investigators** have recorded **disembodied** voices saying, “Go away!” and “I’ll kill you!”

Today, Pennhurst is a haunted **attraction**. People visit to take photographs and explore.

Phantom Swing

Firmat Playground, Santa Fe, Argentina

The small city of Firmat is known for farming—and a haunted swing!

In one of the city's playgrounds, there is a swing that has a life of its own. It moves back and forth all by itself. It swings and swings for 10 days at a time and then stops. Soon after, it suddenly starts again!

Playground in Firmat

When they first saw the swing move, the people of Firmat were **baffled**. Scientists couldn't explain what was happening. Many locals believe the ghost of a little boy is moving the swing. He died in an accident at the playground when it was being built. Is his spirit still there, swinging for **eternity**?

People have tried to stop the swing from moving. But as soon as they let go, it slowly starts swinging again.

Haunted Playgrounds Around the World

Fox Ridge Playground
Henderson, Nevada

Catch a glimpse of the vanishing demon child.

Pennhurst State School and Hospital Playground
Spring City, Pennsylvania

Explore what's left of this haunted playground.

Dead Children's Playground
Huntsville, Alabama

Find out who the spirits are that haunt this site.

Firmat Playground
Santa Fe, Argentina

Check out a swing that never stops swinging.

Glossary

attraction (uh-TRAK-shun) a place that draws visitors

baffled (BA-fuhld) confused

cemetery (SEM-i-ter-ee) an area of land where dead bodies are buried

demon (DEE-muhn) an evil spirit or the devil

disembodied (dis-im-BOD-eed) separated from, or existing without, the body

eternity (i-TUR-ni-tee) endless time

legend (LEJ-uhnd) a story handed down from long ago that is often based on some facts but cannot be proven true

paranormal investigators (pa-ruh-NOR-muhl in-VEST-uh-gay-torz) people who study events or collect information about things that cannot be scientifically explained

patients (PAY-shunts) people who are getting treatment from a doctor

phantom (FAN-tuhm) a ghost or spirit

psychiatric (sye-kee-AT-rik) relating to mental illness or its treatment

INDEX

READ MORE

Markovics, Joyce. *Chilling Cemeteries (Tiptoe Into Scary Places).* New York: Bearport (2017).

Markovics, Joyce. *Eerie Parks and Playgrounds (Scary Places).* New York: Bearport (2019).

LEARN MORE ONLINE

1. Go to **www.factsurfer.com**
2. Enter "**Haunted Playgrounds**" into the search box.
3. Click on the cover of this book to see a list of websites.

ABOUT THE AUTHOR

Rachel Rose lives in San Francisco. Growing up in Ireland, she played in many playgrounds. None of them were haunted. Or so she thought . . .